First Verses
for the
Very Young

Chosen by JOHN FOSTER

Illustrated by
CAROL THOMPSON

OXFORD
UNIVERSITY PRESS

Acknowledgements

We are grateful to the following for permission to publish their poems for the first time in this collection:

Moira Andrew: 'Hush-a-Bye Dragon', Copyright © Moira Andrew 1998. **John Foster:** 'Scuttle Like a Crab', 'In the Middle of the Night', 'The Slippery Soap Song', 'You Can't Catch Me', 'Dad's Cooking Pancakes', 'Tastes', and 'I Like Sizzling Sausages', all Copyright © John Foster 1998. **Carolyn Graham:** 'I Saw a Rabbit' and 'I Hate Spinach', both Copyright © Carolyn Graham 1998. **Julie Holder:** 'A Kangaroo', 'Farmyard Count', and 'Goodnight', all Copyright © Julie Holder 1998. **Mike Jubb:** 'I'm a Giraffe', 'The Bedtime Cuddle Rhyme', 'Plum, Peach, Pineapple, Pear', 'Beans', 'The Playtime Puddle Rhyme', and 'Bouncing Round the Playground', all Copyright © Mike Jubb 1998. **Patricia Leighton:** 'Time For Bed', Copyright © Patricia Leighton 1998. **Wes Magee:** 'Washing-up', 'Six Sweets', 'Books at Bedtime', and 'Who's in Bed?', all Copyright © Wes Magee 1998. **Trevor Millum:** 'My Colouring Book', Copyright © Trevor Millum 1998. **Tony Mitton:** 'Bedtime, Bedtime', 'My Crocodile', 'Dreams', 'The Ball Song', 'Playdough People', 'Hunting For Treasure', 'One Last Go', and 'Bubblegum Balloon', all Copyright © Tony Mitton 1998. **Judith Nicholls:** 'Bedtime, Please' and 'What the Bubble Said', both Copyright © Judith Nicholls 1998. **Paul Rogers:** 'Archibald the Spider', Copyright © Paul Rogers 1998. **Roger Stevens:** 'Last One Back', Copyright © Roger Stevens 1998. **Marian Swinger:** 'A Nature Walk', 'Ball Games', and 'A Munching Monster', all Copyright © Marian Swinger 1998. **Jill Townsend:** 'Elephant Antics' and 'Copycat', both Copyright © Jill Townsend 1998. **Jennifer Tweedie:** 'Boo!', Copyright © Jennifer Tweedie 1998. **Kaye Umansky:** 'Clumsy Clementina' and 'Bed's Best', both Copyright © Kaye Umansky 1998, reprinted by permission of the author ᶜ/o Caroline Sheldon Literary Agency. **Celia Warren:** 'Landscape' and 'Grandma', also both copyright © Celia Warren 1998. **Clive Webster:** 'One Little Sparrow', Copyright © Clive Webster 1998.

We also acknowledge the following previously published poems:

John Agard: 'Skipping Rope Spell' from No Hickory No Dickory No Dock by John Agard and Grace Nicholls (Viking, 1991), Copyright © John Agard 1991, and 'Snow-cone' from I Din Do Nuttin by John Agard (Bodley Head, 1979), reprinted by permission of the author ᶜ/o Caroline Sheldon Literary Agency. **Tony Bradman:** 'Tee, hi, ho, hum', first published by Heinemann in A Kiss on the Nose, Copyright © 1985 Tony Bradman, reprinted by permission of The Agency (London) Ltd. All rights reserved and enquiries to The Agency, 24 Pottery Lane, London W11 4LZ. **Marie Brookes:** 'My Goldfish', Copyright © Marie Brookes 1991, first published in Pet Poems (Oxford Reading Tree), reprinted by permission of the author. **John Coldwell:** 'When the Giant Comes to Breakfast', Copyright © John Coldwell 1992, first published in One In a Million edited by Moira Andrews (Viking Kestrel, 1992), reprinted by permission of the author. **Sheree Fitch:** 'Zelba Zinnamon', from Toes in My Nose, Copyright © 1987 by Sheree Fitch, reprinted by permission of the publishers, Doubleday, Canada Ltd. **John Foster:** 'Poppadoms, Poppadoms', Copyright © John Foster 1991, first published in Food Poems (OUP, 1991), reprinted by permission of the author. **Carolyn Graham:** 'Little Miss Myrtle', Copyright © Carolyn Graham 1994, first published in Mother Goose Jazz Chants (OUP, New York, 1994), reprinted by permission of the author. **Tony Mitton:** 'Hamish the Hamster', first published on 'Pets' poster for Scholastic Infants Projects, and 'The Egg Song', first published in Child Education magazine (Scholastic), both Copyright © Tony Mitton, reprinted here by permission of the author. **Jack Ousbey:** 'Ducks on the Water' and 'Magical Song', first published in Tots TV magazine (Fleetway, 1994), and 'Hair Washing Night', first published in a slightly different form in Poems from the Sac Magique by Jack Ousbey (Scholastic, 1994), all Copyright © Jack Ousbey 1994, reprinted here by permission of the author.

Contents

Animal Rhymes

Playtime Rhymes

Food Rhymes

Bedtime Rhymes

Animal Rhymes

Scuttle Like a Crab

Scuttle like a crab. Creep like a snail. Swim like a dolphin. Dive like a whale.

Stalk like a lion. Pounce like a cat. Jump like a kangaroo. Run like a rat.

Wriggle like a worm. Hop like a frog. Wag your tail and pant like a dog!

John Foster

Archibald the Spider

Spin spin spinning
Web across the air,
Archibald the spider
Scuttles here and there.

Don't move a muscle:
That's what counts.
Archibald the spider
Waiting to pounce.

Here comes a visitor.
Can't afford to miss.
Archibald the spider
Leaps like . . . THIS!

Paul Rogers

Little Miss Myrtle

Little Miss Myrtle sat on a turtle,
Thinking that it was a chair;
'Oww eee!' cried the turtle,
'I'm sorry,' said Myrtle,
'I didn't know you were there.'

Carolyn Graham

A Kangaroo

A kangaroo
One afternoon
Jumped so high
It jumped over the moon!

It jumped so far
It jumped so high
It bumped its head
Upon the sky.

Down it fell
Spinning round
And bumped its bottom
On the ground.

Julie Holder

11

13

Elephant Antics

One little elephant
sitting on a bunk.
Along came another one
and pulled his trunk!

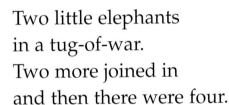

Two little elephants
in a tug-of-war.
Two more joined in
and then there were four.

Four *more* came along,
so there were eight
pulling and tugging
with all their weight.

They all fell over.
And guess what happened then.
They jumped up
and started all over again.

Jill Townsend

14

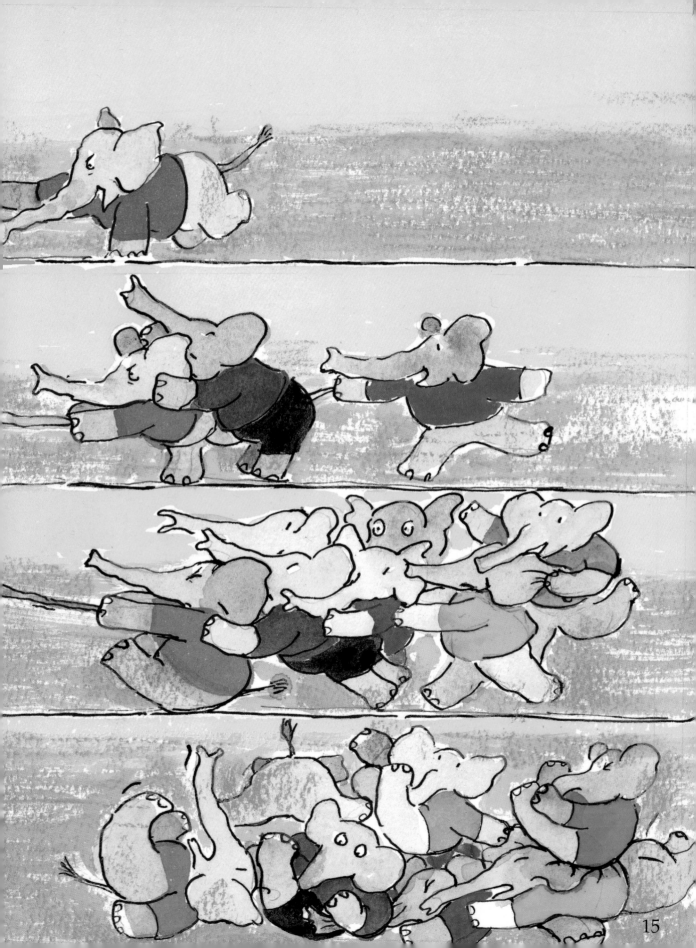

17

Ducks on the Water

Ducks on the water,
    quack,
    quack,
    quack!
Sailing down the river
And then sailing back.

Mother duck leads,
Ducklings behind,
Trim little swimmers
    in
    a
    long
    straight
    line.

Out of the river,
Into the nest.
Time for the family
To have a rest.

Under her wings
Mother duck tucks
Two little drakes
        and
Three little ducks.

Jack Ousbey

Hamish the Hamster

There's a scrabble and a scratch.
There's a scuffle and a squeal.
It's Hamish the Hamster
On his exercise wheel.

There's a nibble and a gnaw.
There's a crackle and a crunch.
It's hungry Hamish Hamster
Chewing up his lunch.

Tony Mitton

My Goldfish

My goldfish is the perfect pet.
She isn't any trouble.
She doesn't bark,
She doesn't mew,
   just bubble
      bubble
         bubbles.

My goldfish is the perfect pet.
She isn't any trouble.
We don't have to feed her much,
She doesn't need a rabbit hutch,
   just bubble
      bubble
         bubbles.

Marie Brookes

21

One Little Sparrow

One little sparrow
Pecking at the crumbs.
One beak pecking,
Then another comes.

Two little sparrows
Pecking at the crumbs.
Two beaks pecking,
Then another comes.

Three little sparrows
Pecking at the crumbs.
Three beaks pecking,
Then a pussy comes.

No little sparrows
Pecking at the crumbs.
Sparrows don't like pussies—
They fly off to their mums.

One little pussy cat.
Now there are two.
Now there's a third one
Coming into view.

Three little pussy cats,
Soon there'll be none.
A doggy comes and barks.
Away they all run.

Clive Webster

The Egg Song

Peck, peck, peck,
went the little chick's beak.
Out poked its head
as it took a little peek.

Out stepped its leg.
Out flapped its wing.
Then the fluffy yellow chick
began to sing:

'Take me to the water.
Show me to the seed.
If I'm going to live and grow,
that is what I'll need.

'Then when I'm a chicken,
feathery and grown,
I can cluck and lay an egg
all of my own.'

Tony Mitton

The Cuckoo Calls

The cuckoo calls, coo, coo, coo,
Don't touch the mangoes any of you,
For I am the mango queen you see,
Eating mangoes is for me.

Traditional Indian

A Nature Walk

One for the rabbit who nibbled the hay.
Two for the field-mice who scuttled away.
Three for the weasels with beady black eyes.
Four for the frogs in the pond catching flies.
Five for the foxes with fine bushy tails.
Six for the slugs with their silvery trails.
Seven for the skylarks who sang in the sky.
Eight for the squirrels who scampered by.
Nine for the hedgehogs who shuffled around.
Ten for the badgers who hid underground.

Marian Swinger

Farmyard Count

One for a baa
Two for a moo
Three for a flap and a cock-a-doodle-doo
Four for an oink
Five for hee-haw
Six for a squeak and a rustle in the straw
Seven for a neigh
Eight for a bark
Nine for a hoot in the barn roof dark
Ten for a quack
Eleven for meow
Twelve for the farmyard
ALL TOGETHER NOW! . . .

Julie Holder

Playtime Rhymes

The Ball Song

Throw me up and catch me,
bounce me on the ground,
put me down and twist me,
twizzle me around.

Drop me on the floor,
kick me at the wall.
Bounce me! Bounce me!
I'm a bouncy ball.

Tony Mitton

6 · 7 · 8 · 9 · 10

What the Bubble Said

You can't catch me!
said the bubble.
See that tree?
I can fly to the top!

Oh no you can't,
said the blackbird.
See this beak?
I can make you

POP!

Judith Nicholls

Hush-a-Bye Dragon

Hush-a-bye Dragon
on a kite-tail,
when the wind blows
the dragon will sail.

When the wind stops,
the kite-tail will swoop,
down will come Dragon
looping-the-loop.

Moira Andrew

33

Playdough People

Playdough people
are floppy and fat.
Some wear a funny old
playdough hat.

Playdough people
have playdough faces,
with blobs for noses
and hair like laces.

Playdough people
have bendy legs,
ears like pancakes,
eyes like eggs.

Playdough people
roll up in a ball.
Then playdough people
aren't people at all.

Tony Mitton

35

My Colouring Book

There's a letter-box
In my colouring book.
I've coloured it red.
Come and look.

There's a little chick
In my colouring book.
I've coloured it yellow.
Come and look.

There's a Christmas tree
In my colouring book.
I've coloured it green.
Come and look.

There's a big fat cat
In my colouring book.
I've coloured it purple.
Come and look.

Trevor Millum

37

Bouncing Round the Playground

Bouncing round the playground
Like a kangaroo;
We're going to Australia,
You can come too.

Waddling round the playground
Like the penguins do;
We're going to the South Pole,
You can come too.

Whizzing round the playground
Like a rocket ship;
We're going to the Milky Way . . .
Have a good trip.

Mike Jubb

Hunting For Treasure

This is my treasure map.
This is my boat.
These are the waves
where I rock and float.

There is the island
I'm headed for.
This is the way
that I wade ashore.

40

This is the spot.
This is my spade.
This is the deep,
dark hole I made.

This is the box
that I dug from the ground.
And these are the golden
coins I found.

Tony Mitton

41

You Can't Catch Me!

I chased Tina.
Tina chased Lee.
Lee chased Pat.
Pat chased me.

In and out the bushes.
Round and round the tree.
Up and down the path.
You can't catch me!

I chased Pat.
Pat chased Lee.
Lee chased Tina.
Tina chased me.

John Foster

The Playtime Puddle Rhyme

Puddle, splash, puddle, splash,
Don't go near the puddle, splash.
You'll get into trouble, splash,
So don't go near the puddle—SPLASH!

Mike Jubb

43

Skipping Rope Spell

Turn rope turn
don't trip my feet.
Turn rope turn
for my skipping feet.

Turn rope turn
turn round and round.
Turn in the air
turn on the ground.

One for your high
one for your low.
Turn rope turn
not too fast, not too slow.

Turn rope turn
turn to the north
turn to the south.
But please, rope, please,
don't make me out.

John Agard

45

Copycat

Copy everything I do.
Me first, then you.

Hold your hands up.
Scratch your head.

Point to something
that is red.

Jump about.
Then be a tree.

Be a teapot
full of tea.

Be a balloon
about to burst.
All right—now
you go first.

Jill Townsend

Boo!

Hop on one foot,
Jump on two,
Turn right round
And shout out
Boo!

Jennifer Tweedie

One Last Go

I know it's time to go now.
I know it's time, I know.
But please, Dad; please, Dad,
Can I have one last go?

One more go on the see-saw.
One more go on the swing.
One more go on the roundabout.
One more on everything.

One more go on the climbing-frame.
One more go on the slide.
One more go on the motor-bike.
One last ride!

Tony Mitton

Last One Back

Stand on one leg
Touch your nose
Jump for the sky
And land on your toes
Run for the climbing frame
Run for the tree
The last one back
Is a chimpanzee

Roger Stevens

Food Rhymes

I Like Sizzling Sausages

I like sizzling sausages.   I like bubbling beans.

I like cauliflower cheese
And all kinds of greens.

I like hot tomato soup.   I like chicken wings.

I like crisp fish fingers.
I like spaghetti rings.

I like eggs and bacon.
And Mum's potato cakes.

But most of all I really like
The fresh bread my gran bakes.

John Foster

Landscape

My potato is an island.
The gravy is the sea.
The peas are people swimming;
The biggest one is me.

My carrots are whales
That make the sea wavy,
But the big brown blobs
Are LUMPS in the gravy!

Celia Warren

Plum, Peach, Pineapple, Pear

Plum, peach, pineapple, pear,
I could eat you anywhere;

Pear, plum, pineapple, peach,
Come for a picnic on the beach;

Peach, pear, pineapple, plum,
Hurry up and give me some!

Mike Jubb

Little Jack Horner

Little Jack Horner sat in a corner,
Eating his Christmas Pie.
He put in his thumb,
And pulled out a plum,
And squirted the juice in his eye.

Anon

55

Tastes

Jelly's slippery.

Ice-cream's cold.

Toffee's sweet
And sticky to hold.

Curry is hot
And full of spice.

Crisps are crunchy.

Chocolate's nice.

John Foster

Snow-cone

Snow-cone nice
snow-cone sweet
snow-cone is crush ice
and good for the heat.

When sun really hot
and I thirsty a lot,
me alone,
yes, me alone,
could eat ten snow-cone.

If you think is lie I tell
wait till you hear the snow-cone bell,
wait till you hear the snow-cone bell.

John Agard

Zelba Zinnamon

Zelba Zinnamon
She loved cinnamon
She loved cinnamon cake
Zelba Zinnamon
Ate so much cinnamon
She got a bellyache

Then Zelba Zinnamon
Sniffed the cinnamon
Got her nose all red
Zelba Zinnamon
Nose full of cinnamon
Had to go to bed.

Sheree Fitch

Clumsy Clementina

Clumsy Clementina
Tripped over the cat.
Up flew her ice cream,
Oops!
Bump!
Splat!
Cone in her ear,
Ice-cream on her clothes,
And a chocolate flake
Up
Her
Nose!

Kaye Umansky

I Hate Spinach

I hate spinach
I hate salt
I can't help it
It's not my fault.

I like sugar
I like tea
I like things that start with 'c'
Cookies, candy, chocolate cakes
I like the things that my mum bakes.

Carolyn Graham

Poppadoms, Poppadoms

Poppadoms, poppadoms,
with chicken and rice.
Poppadoms, poppadoms,
plain or spice.
Crispy hot poppadoms
to crunch and chew.
A plateful of poppadoms
for me and you.

John Foster

Beans

Beans on bread,
Beans on toast;
Beans are what I love the most.

Beans in a pie,
Beans in a stew;
Beans are what I love to chew.

Beans and chips,
Beans and fish;
Beans are such a lovely dish.

Beans with veg,
Beans with meat;
Beans are what I want to eat.

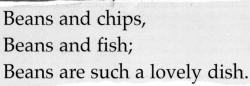

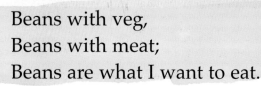

Beans in a bun,
Beans in a roll,
Beans in a sandwich,
Beans in the hole,
Beans in a trifle,
Beans in a mousse,
Beans in lemonade,
Beans in juice,
Beans in a crumble,
Beans in a cake,
Beans in a cola,
Beans in a shake,
Beans with custard,
Beans with cream,
Give me beans, or I will SCREAM.

Mike Jubb

Dad's Cooking Pancakes

Dad's cooking pancakes for our tea—
One for you, one for you, and one for me.

Stir the batter in the bowl.
Mix. Mix. Mix.
Stir up all the flour and eggs.
Whisk. Whisk. Whisk.

Fry the batter in the pan.
Fry.   Fry.   Fry.
Toss the pancake in the air.
High.   High.   High.

Put the pancake on your plate,
Crisp and golden brown.
Sprinkle it with sugar
And gobble it down!

John Foster

Bubblegum Balloon

Bubblegum, bubblegum,
big pink balloon.

Bubblegum, bubblegum,
round like the moon.

Bubblegum, bubblegum,
planet in space.

Bubblegum bursting
in my face!

Tony Mitton

Six Sweets

Six sweets in a paper bag.
Shake them up and down.

Six sweets in a paper bag.
Shake them round and round.

R I P !

No sweets in a paper bag.
They're all on the ground!

Pick them up . . .

One
     Two
   Three
       Four
Five
   Six!

Wes Magee

Gingerbread Man

'Gingerbread's too hard,'
  said the Gingerbread Man,
'I'd rather be made of marzipan.'

'Marzipan's too soft,'
  said the Marzipan Man,
'I'd rather be made of strawberry jam.'

'Strawberry jam's too runny,'
  said the Strawberry Jam Man,
'I'd rather be made of plain meringue.'

'Meringue's too stiff,'
  the Meringue Man said,
'I'd rather be made of gingerbread!'

Celia Warren

69

A Munching Monster

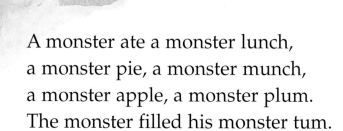

A monster ate a monster lunch,
a monster pie, a monster munch,
a monster apple, a monster plum.
The monster filled his monster tum.

He licked a monster lollipop.
He drank a bottle of monster pop.
He chomped a monster chocolate cake
and got a monster stomach ache.

Marian Swinger

When the Giant Comes to Breakfast

When the giant comes to breakfast,
He eats cornflakes with a spade,
Followed by a lorry-load
Of toast and marmalade.

Next, he takes a dustbin,
Fills it up with tea,
Drinks it all in a gulp
And leaves the mess for me.

John Coldwell

Washing-Up

Wash the spoons,
Wash the forks,
Wash each plate and cup.
Put your hands
In soapy suds
And do the washing-up.

Wash the pots,
Wash the pans,
Make them squeaky clean.
You're a splishy,
Splashy, sploshy
Washing-up machine!

Wes Magee

Bedtime Rhymes

Bedtime, Bedtime

Bedtime, bedtime,
that's-what-Daddy-said-time.

Bedtime, bedtime,
stories-to-be-read-time.

Bedtime, bedtime,
cuddle-up-with-Ted-time.

Bedtime, bedtime,
rest-my-sleepy-head-time.

Bedtime, bedtime,
sssssssssshhhhhhhh . . .

Tony Mitton

Bedtime, Please!

One, two,
off with that shoe!
Three, four,
socks on the floor!
Five, six,
no more tricks!
Seven, eight,
you are LATE!
Nine, ten,
I won't tell you again!

Judith Nicholls

Before the Bath

It's cold, cold, cold
And the water shines wet,
And the longer I wait
The colder I get.

I can't quite make
Myself hop in
All shivery-cold
In just my skin.

Yet the water's warm
In the tub, I know
So—one, two, three,
And IN I go!

Corinna Marsh

The Slippery Soap Song

It slips through your fingers.
It slides, slides, slides
Under the water where
It hides, hides, hides.

Slippery soap,
Slippery soap,
You haven't a hope
Of catching the soap.

It slips through your hands.
It glides, glides, glides
Down towards the taps where
It hides, hides, hides.

Slippery soap,
Slippery soap,
You haven't a hope
Of catching the soap.

John Foster

Hair-Washing Night

Here comes Jason,
Here comes John;
Here comes Joey
With his rain-hat on.

John's big towel
Is fluffy and blue,
Jason has a bottle
Of yellow shampoo.

John has a brush,
Jason has a comb
And very special soap
In the shape of a gnome.

Under goes Jason,
Under goes John;
Under goes Joey
With his rain-hat on.

Scrub-a-rub one head,
Rub-a-dub two;
Soap suds flying—
Yellow shampoo.

'Jason,' says John,
'Just look at that.
Joey's hair's still
Under his hat.'

Out goes Jason,
Out goes John;
Out goes Joey
With his rain-hat on.

Jack Ousbey

79

Time For Bed

No more telly,
time to go to bed.

Climb the stairs slowly,
tread by tread.

Go to the bathroom,
clean your teeth.

Before you climb into bed
look underneath!

Jump in bed with teddy,

hold him tight.

Say 'goodnight' three times for luck

and switch
off
the light.

Patricia Leighton

81

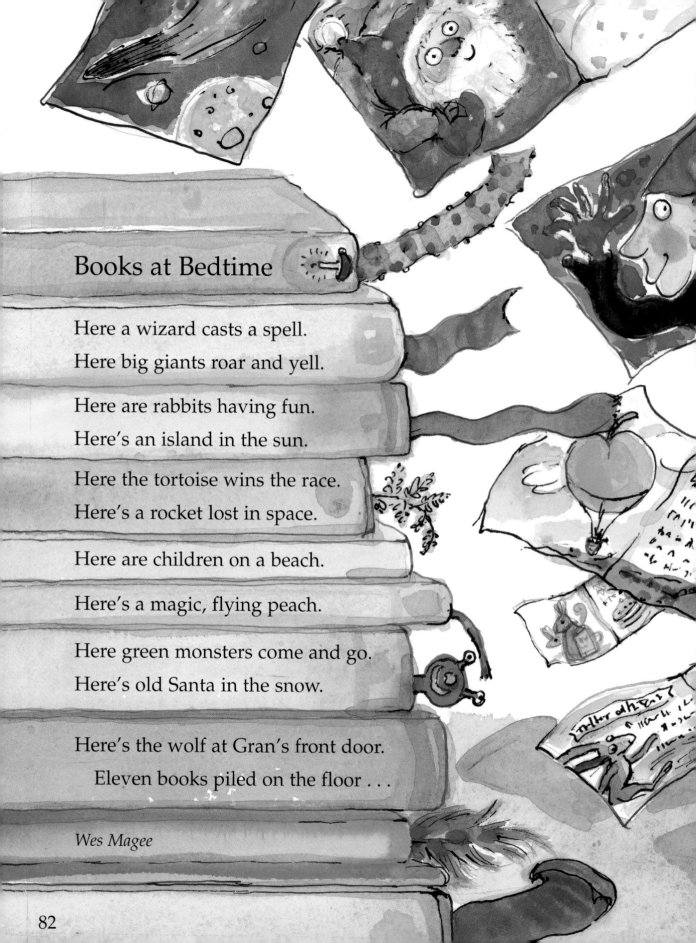

Books at Bedtime

Here a wizard casts a spell.
Here big giants roar and yell.

Here are rabbits having fun.
Here's an island in the sun.

Here the tortoise wins the race.
Here's a rocket lost in space.

Here are children on a beach.

Here's a magic, flying peach.

Here green monsters come and go.
Here's old Santa in the snow.

Here's the wolf at Gran's front door.
   Eleven books piled on the floor . . .

Wes Magee

Bed's Best

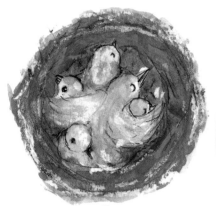
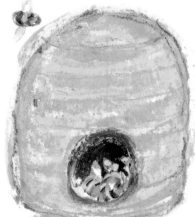

A nest is best for a bird,
A hive is best for a bee,
Moles and voles
Are best in holes

But bed's the best
for me.

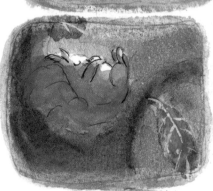

A cat can nap on a mat,
A squirrel can curl in a tree,
Fish have dreams
In ponds and streams

But bed's the best
for me.

84

A sheep can sleep in a field,
A cow is best in a shed,

But teddy and me,
We both agree,

We like it best in bed.

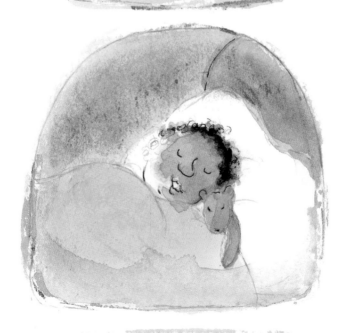

Kaye Umansky

Who's in Bed?

Who's tucked-up
　　with me in bed?
Peter Panda,
　　One-eared Ted,
Steady Freddy,
　　Wizard Mac,
Floppy Dog
　　and Jumping Jack.
Silly Snake
　　and Pirate Smee
all tucked-up
　　in bed with me!

Wes Magee

The Bedtime Cuddle Rhyme

Cuddle me, cuddle me, cuddle me tight,
Kiss me when you say, 'Goodnight';
Then just as you turn out the light,
Cuddle me, cuddle me, cuddle me tight.

Mike Jubb

Goodnight

Goodnight goodnight
Sleepy head
Throw back the covers
And roll into bed.
Wink at the stars
Wave at the moon
Close your eyes now
You'll be fast asleep soon.

Julie Holder

Fee, Fi, Fo, Fum

Fee, fi, fo, fum,
Look out in there—
Here I come!

If you're awake
And not asleep,
Under the bedclothes
I will creep.

If you're awake
And not asleep,
I'll tickle your toes
Till I make you squeak!

Fee, fi, fo, fum,
Look out in there—
Here I come!

Tony Bradman

My Crocodile

My crocodile is very small.
He has no claws or teeth at all.
He doesn't scratch.
He doesn't bite.
He's safe to take to bed at night.

For when he's there, I'm glad to say,
He helps to snap bad dreams away.

Tony Mitton

Dreams

I dreamed of a dragon
with big, sharp claws.
I dreamed of a giant
with great, loud roars.
I dreamed of a monster
who asked me to play.
Then when I woke up
they all went away.

Tony Mitton

In the Middle of the Night

In the middle of the night
When you are sleeping,
Who comes creeping?
Who comes peeping?

Mouse comes creeping.
Mouse comes peeping.

Cat comes creeping.
Cat comes peeping.

In the middle of the night
When you are sleeping.
Who comes creeping?
Who comes peeping?

Mum comes creeping.
Mum comes peeping.
Shoos away the mouse.
Shoos away the cat.
Tucks you in
And leaves you
Soundly
          soundly
                    soundly
Sleeping.

John Foster

Magical Song

If you listen at night
When you put out the light,
And the moonshine comes into your room;
At the end of the day
You may hear, faraway,
A magical, musical tune.

And the tune someone's playing
Will seem to be saying,
It's time to be counting out sheep;
This magical song
Doesn't last very long,
It ends as you're falling asleep.

Jack Ousbey

Index of Titles and First Lines

First lines are shown in italics

Index of Authors

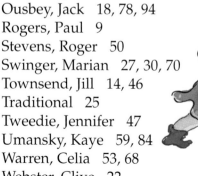